Daniel Gómez

TO LIVE TO THE FULLEST EVERY DAY.

Daniel Gómez.
dango
@ccdango

Photography and images: Javier Nava.
Design and production: Edson Gomez N.

ASIN: B0107H9A4C

Check and update in May 2016.

Original language: Spanish
Translation to English: No Native

Mérida; Venezuela. 2015-2016

To live to the fullest every day.

Dear Friend: Do not expect to meet a self-help book or self-improvement, because in reality this book contains a photographic sample of thirty one image of beautiful landscapes of the region of Los Andes in Venezuela, each accompanied by a short story, reflective thought or quote, that when you finish reading them hope to fulfill our purpose, to contribute in some way and somehow for you, be a better person and live to the fullest every day.

"He who lives in harmony with himself lives in harmony with the universe." Marcus Aurelius.

To live to the fullest every day.

This book is not intended in any way be a text self-help or self-improvement, of those many that are published daily and you've maybe read by dozens, where you compare with other species of our animal kingdom and you suggest that act like them to improve yourself or those other books invent a tale that ultimately do not know whether or not to believe, which ends giving more concern.

Nor it is one of those books that make you follow a recipe similar to a menu gourmet that treaty improvement.

No, absolutely not; that was not the intention to translate this writing, just wanted to show something different, an experience of those now called multimedia, which contemplate that wonderful mix of images, videos, sounds and text, revolving around a particular subject, but as for make a multimedia product, programming, compiling, deep layout and a team is needed, we present it is; multimedia our proposal, "a proposal that combines images and text," where he managed to unite the wonderful photographic collection, captured by the photographer Javier young adventurer Alexander Nava; one of the best photographers of natural landscapes that proudly has Venezuela, framed in the region of the Venezuelan Andes and composed of thirty-one images, each accompanied by a short story, thought or reflective event, which develop different lines of life, that in adopting to them to their liking, surely it will provide some important training to live the most of every day of that wonderful gift called element: **LIFE.**

To live to the fullest every day.

You can perfectly read each day of the month, the story, thought or quote, while of delight with the image that accompanies it, as often as desired to generate thirty-one different experiences.

The book can be read in full in two or three days, because we believe that in addition to not be very extensive, it is very pleasant to read or as we suggest above, you can read it daily so that I interacted and reflect on each point It arises.

Make the most of the images, which are not only beautiful for the quality of photographic work and presented landscapes but also each invited to reflect in peace and meditate until tranquility.

If you want and have the opportunity, we extend a friendly invitation to visit the Venezuelan Andes region comprising the states of Táchira, Merida and Trujillo, where he also get beautiful natural scenery, friendly people, serenity and all necessary services to enjoy your stay.

Stay that will surely allow you to find a magical place that connects it fully with nature so that when you return to your everyday life how to do better and more complete person. Warn once again, without being a traditional book of self-help or self-improvement, we sincerely hope that when you finish reading it, be a better person, to his joy, happiness of his friends, for the benefit of their country, to hope world and especially to be at peace with that Superior Force undoubtedly guide us: **To live to the fullest every day.**

The Author.

First day: Admiration and friendship.

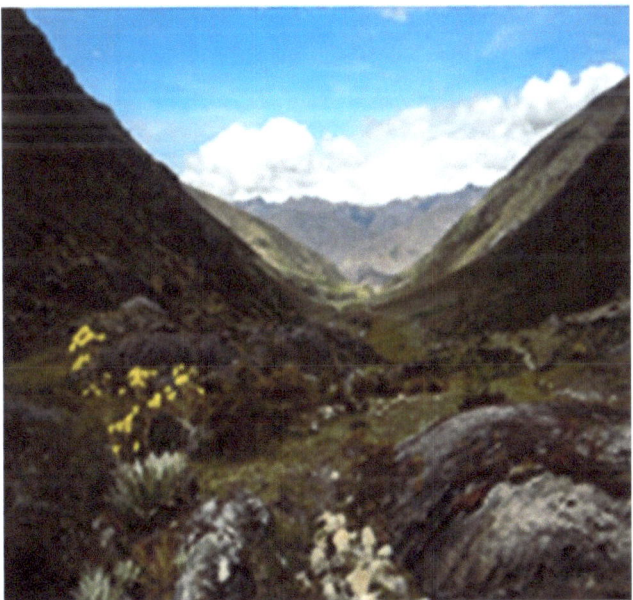

View from the path of the lagoon El Hoyo; Merida, Venezuela.

Admire the characters who have acted with courage, honor and honesty in difficult situations, imagine those relevant beings in history that have marked their actions the fate of our world, consider those experts in the area that needs attention and these experts think they would if they were at his side in a difficult situation.

This will make you act with wisdom and courage, however; Always remember two important things: Do not try to compare at any time or under any situation with others, because everyone must live his life acting as dictated by his own conscience and the wisdom gained through their experiences.

But if you can take it as a model, as an inspiration, also remember; with special significance that friend of his childhood, growing up with you, which was part of your family, your father and your mother considered another son to him; remember it very special way, remember the moments when they played and were accomplices in mischief, how escaping a difficult situation or could that every day despite any difficulty him smile, that remember it when new friends circumventing a difficult situation, because true and lasting friendship usually comes from childhood.

Organize with his friends a solid team aimed at achieving a common aim; and they have certainly done for fun on more than one occasion, organize them into a team where allowed to take and share responsibility at any stage of the projects they undertake.

Note that in addition to making work more enjoyable and less complicated experience; since you will not have major problems in labor relations, the goals will be easier to get because it will be a fun adventure with a pleasant and reliable company.

"Two things fill me with the spirit of admiration: The starry sky above me and the moral law itself." Immanuel Kant; German philosopher. Precursor of Idealism in Germany and throughout Europe.

Second day: The art of giving a gift.

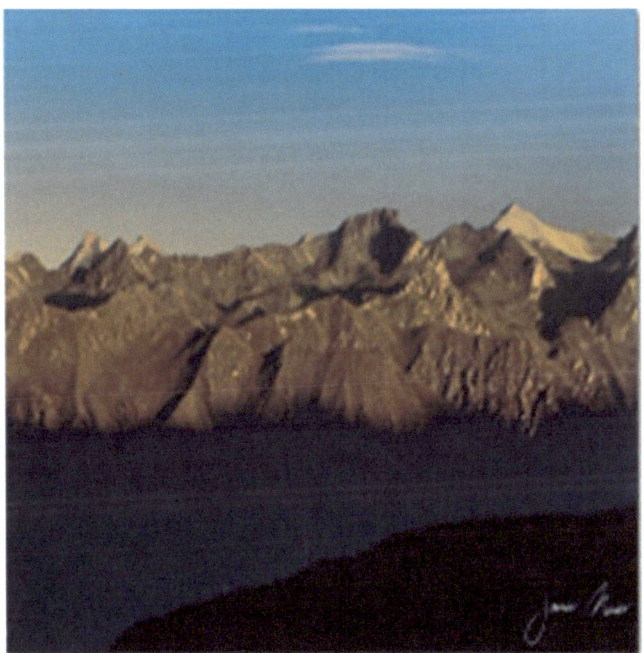

Dawn at Pan de Azucar; Merida, Venezuela.

Give others the best of himself at all times, do not need to have large amounts of money or going to the most luxurious store in town to buy the most expensive gift from the main showcase for the purpose of gifting it, use your besides creativity to exercise your mind positively, convert to an art.

A simple card, a card with a sincere dedication friendship, a phone message to a friend or a simple smile support for someone who needs it, it will be enough for you and someone else are for a happy moment and that simple action will spread too many other of happiness you enjoy.

Keep in mind that every morning at the same time to open your eyes there is a wonderful gift waiting for him, because life is a wonderful gift and every day must decide what you want to do with your gift, whatever the circumstance to face, should open your gift with immense gratitude and hope for a rebirth, knowing he has just opposite the ability to start in the best way possible the start of steady progress in his life; every day that gift you receive is an adventure that should start and therefore you should be aware: **To live to the fullest every day.**

Try conviction and with absolute faith and always be thankful at all times for that gift received daily at sunrise, as you are one of the privileged select who have received the best of gifts: **Life.**

"The best gift we can give another person is our full attention." Richard Moss. Master of conscience. Gives talks and workshops for training and reflection for more than 30 years in various parts of the world.

Third day: Seeking inner peace.

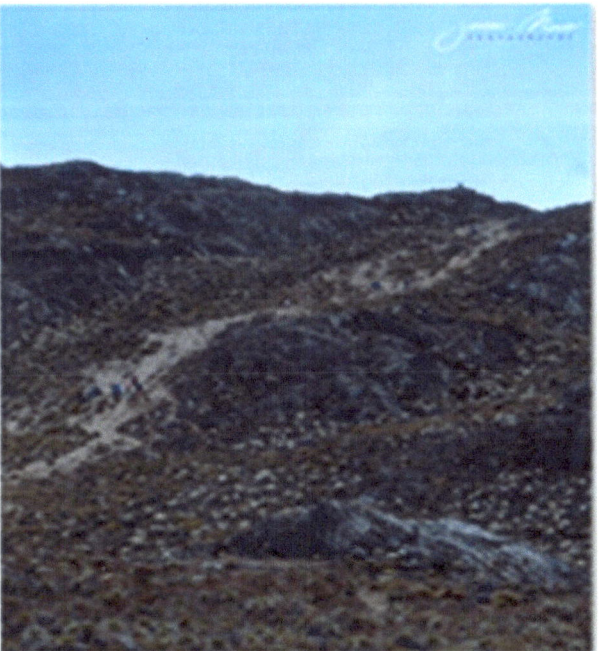

Road to Alto del Santo Cristo; Merida, Venezuela.

Life is a divine energy that flows every day, every moment without stopping, from the very second that a being is begotten until his last breath and possibly beyond; that's why all fortunate to enjoy life we must always be grateful to the universe by the force of the body and by the light of the mind. You should keep in mind that a healthy and strong body with a creative mind, define what is and what you can accomplish during their passage through this life.

Therefore seek to preserve a healthy body and mind acting with discipline, balance and prudence as long as possible.

To live to the fullest every day.

The limitations that your body or mind present at any given time, should seek to heal them immediately, just by detecting an alarm signal will come from your own body, consider eating properly, reduce the consumption of processed foods as industrialized as possible, the milk products; remember that cow's milk is to feed their young, and you do not have the digestive system of a calf, white refined sugar and foods that contain it, they are a potential poison for the pancreas, which through generation enzyme is the body to properly digest fats, carbohydrates and protein you eat, also regulates our energy and take the necessary and adequate levels of blood sugar.

Be careful while increasing consumption of green food, fruit and vegetable juices, smoothies, soups or in its natural presentation, the pancreas to detoxify progressively and cells throughout your body to regenerate, but while that happens must develop serenity of mind and spirit through daily practice of meditation and control of their emotions and breathing rate.

Always remember; that in this world there are people who have severe mobility limitations and are able to solve problems of quantum physics or some others who have mental coordination and still win competitions marathon, confirming the infinite power of the mind and body when they are governed by discipline, balance and prudence.

Only when with absolute sincerity and humility, thank and acknowledge daily with full awareness that the health of your body and mind allows you to meet the challenges the future holds life that skill your body has to work, rest properly, recover and achieve physical and cell regeneration, and that the creative ability that expresses their actions thanks to the alertness. Only at that time; you will find the source of inner peace and serenity necessary to live in harmony.

That will be the true path to take proper action for this wonderful journey called life.

To which I was fortunate to be selected among millions. As soccer player that is just waiting call from coach to represent his country in a World Cup.

"Go down to the depths of yourself, and see your good soul will achieve." Socrates. Greek philosopher, considered one of the greatest of Western and universal philosophy.

Fourth day: Harmony to achieve world peace.

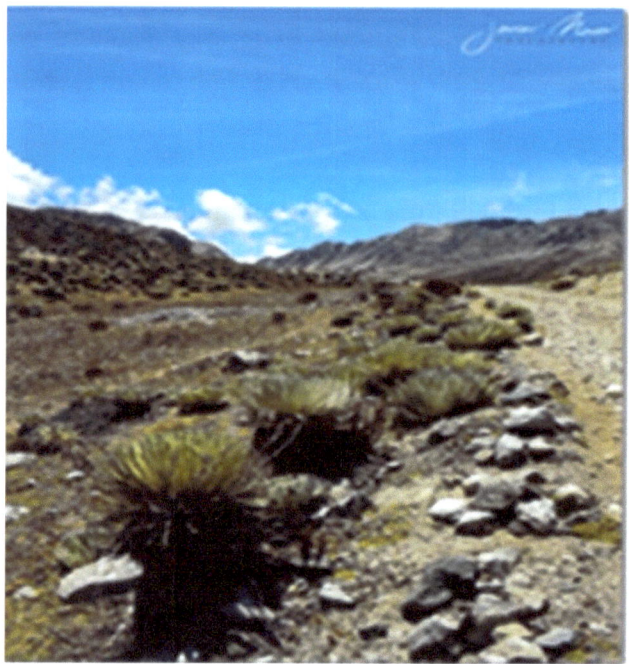

The route Frailejones; Merida, Venezuela.

Always stay in harmony with their thoughts and convictions, ensure that they are at all times and under any circumstance positive thoughts, because they undoubtedly transformed into positive action.

If for some reason, feel fear, anxiety or worry, take a deep breath, observe in silence the vastness and serenity of the sky, discuss the fact that you see all that immensity in perfect peace and harmony, immediately feel your feelings and emotions are stilled and allow you to retrieve the course of their thoughts, actions and life.

When witness acts of discord among people, friends, family, groups or countries understand that despite any religious, racial, gender or idiosyncrasy difference, we are all like a bicycle wheel whose spokes are joining in the center, that center is the same divine source for all despite turning in different directions we will always be attached to the center, which makes it important to part with their shares in a peaceful alternative of life for many.

Any action performed by smaller it affects others in their act, so if your action is certainly positive find answers and positive actions; this is the authentic way to build peace and common growth.

Its mission from this moment, as a responsible adult is to plant every day the seeds of future peace, which is simply to educate children who are noble and innocent souls who are not corrupt unless they receive a bad example, inculcating in them values of respect, solidarity, responsibility, discipline, moral, can fend for this practice sports, fine arts, performing arts, also keep in mind that a child change for the better is a good result for peace future.

"It is not enough to talk about peace. One must believe strongly in it and work every day to get" Eleanor Roosevelt, American diplomatic defender of social rights. Key in the adoption of the Universal Declaration of Human Rights.

Fifth day: Presence for forgiveness.

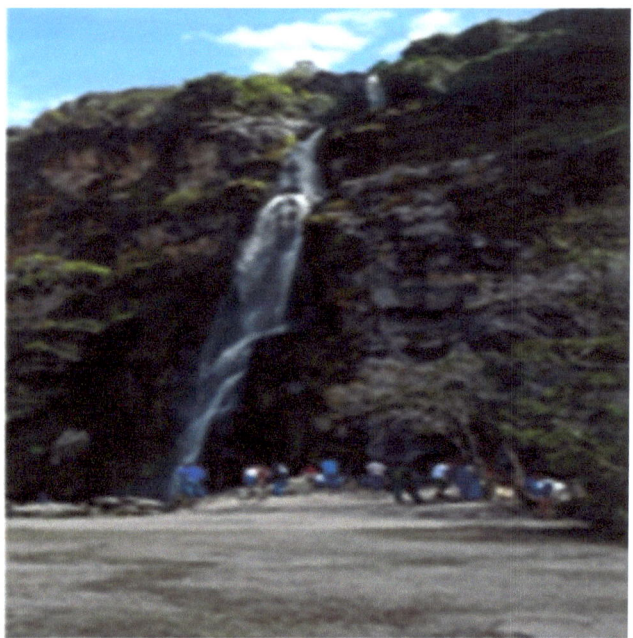
Wine waterfall; Lara, Venezuela.

Living in all consents time of the existence of a higher power, note that you can align positively your thoughts in the pursuit of health, wisdom and harmony, achieving out of his evil thoughts mind based on the errors that come dragging from the past, this allows you born in a new person full of complete happiness.

This upper force accompanying the journey of life, easy to focus their perceptions about past situations where you think that life could have been treated better, allowing you to choose a different perception of that experience, focusing attention on the many blessings received and not worrying about giving importance to insults and offenses for which it could have happened.

That perception makes it easier to put the past behind, but as you learn from those experiences should remember the obligation to forgive and move toward a new future in love and abundance, where the experiences of the past must be only references to reach the road which will take you for a better present and a hopeful future.

Relieves slowly but steadily all wounds and resentments that negative situations left etched in your mind, check the weapons that hurt you and the situation that allowed such weapons attack against you and you'll notice that were only an experience of life , with the divine presence that soon will become learning, giving a new opportunity to make it better but this time, without leaving wounded again.

"Forgiving is not having too much into account offenses, limitations and shortcomings of others, not taken them too seriously, but play it down, and with good disposition saying: I know you're not." Robert Spaemann. German philosopher. Professor at the Universities of Sttugart, Heidelberg and Munich, member of the Pontifical Academy for Life.

Sixth day: Responsibility to bring blessings.

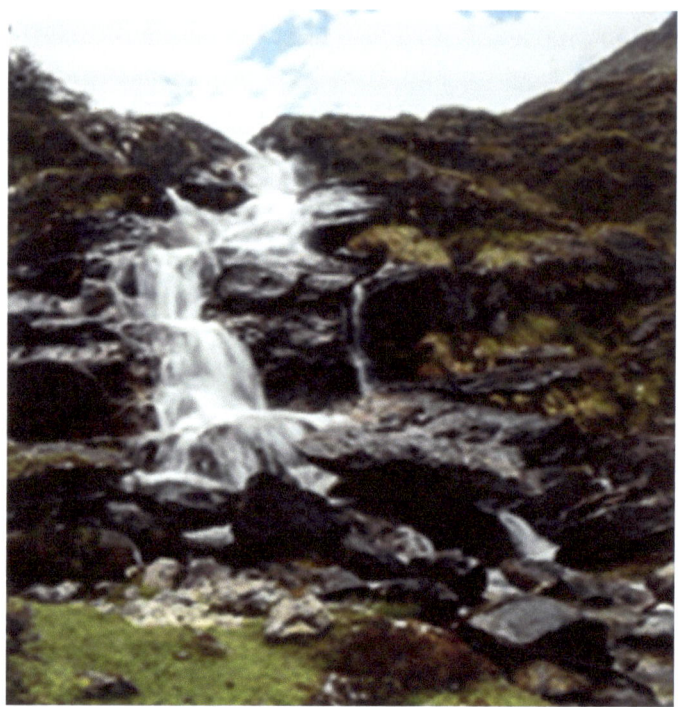

Waterfall El Hoyo; Merida, Venezuela.

When you make mistakes, surely going to make, you should be aware that they are part of learning to cope with life, yes; should strive with all the strength of his heart and mind, not to commit them again, however; You should also know; there are errors that are difficult to overcome and become for you a very high cost.

Keep in mind at that time he has to take responsibility for their actions and the consequences thereof, in order to obtain the divine grace which will make a man faithful to his principles so you live day to day appreciating what it does.

Be aware of the consequences of their actions and take full responsibility for their actions and decisions, all acts made and the decisions you make in life, are solely your responsibility and not blame anyone more than just its exclusive responsibility, because this is nothing but a poor excuse to evade its commitments.

Remember at all times that their decisions and actions present becomes their life and future well-being, with divine guidance and firm conviction, will be aware that everything will be fine, do not rush the march to get the results if that means going to skip some detail, arm yourself with patience and not lose heart; because everything comes at the right time when it is deemed ready to take full responsibility for their challenges and enjoy the fruits of the action that you have undertaken.

"The biggest day of your life is when you take full responsibility for all your actions. That is the day that really grows." John C. Maxwell. Motivational speaker. American. Leadership expert with more than 80 titles published on the subject.

Seventh day: Honesty and integrity.

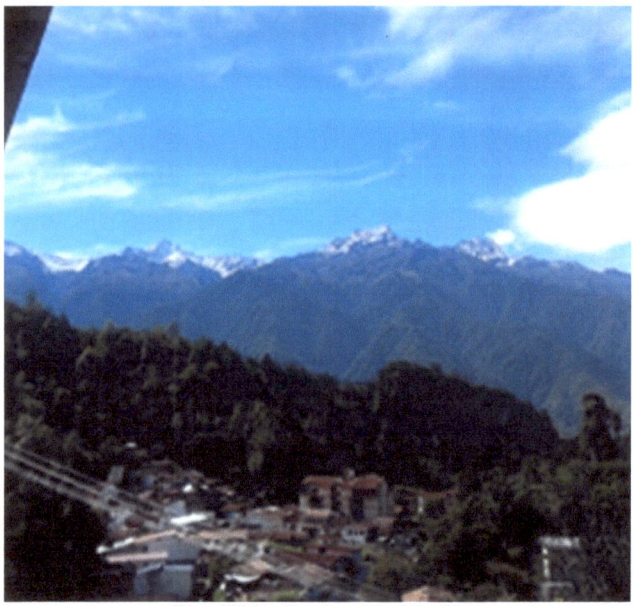
Five White Eagles; Merida, Venezuela.

Remember when he was a boy and his mother sent him to buy food to prepare dinner, you bought everything indicated the list, but when I left some coins change; before leaving the store, he looked thoughtful showcase cookies and chocolates, you knew you could not use the coins to buy what he liked; because despite the desire to eat cookies and chocolates, these coins were not his, always remember that and know that the honest man in little things, when temptation is greater, can be assured that reason be honest.

Take time to do what you know is good for you and those around you without thereby harm anyone, because with that attitude expressed respect, honesty and integrity; that their actions are the moral compass to guide his whole being, because acting with integrity, honesty and respect for others, will soon begin to see how slowly disappear from your life negative thoughts and lose the fear but not respecting face new challenges to it by fate.

Yes; remember that a deal is a deal and must fulfill it regardless, because the word given by a responsible man worth more than any signatures notarized document translated into.

"I hope to always have enough strength and power to keep what I consider the most enviable of all titles: the character of an honest man." George Washington. Military. First President of the United States of America.

Eighth day: Attentive to Happiness.

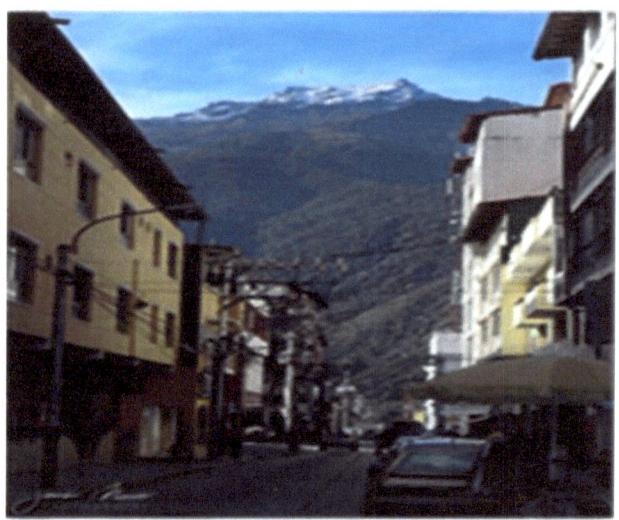

City between mountains; Merida, Venezuela.

Start each morning your day with a huge smile, full of optimism, thanking the universe for this new opportunity it gives you to enjoy life, that happiness remember to share and transmit it to all people who may be known or not, because happiness is a state of mind, body and heart and that daily attitude towards life, happiness may retain for longer.

Should be aware of all the opportunities that are presented daily, however small they may be, as presented by a special reason, in addition you must also be alert to the possibility of selflessly serving others and soon will be rewarded with experiences that will give happiness in any way that is profitable.

Any more uncomfortable or more unexpected situation it is, right there; happiness will come to your life, so do not be troubled; at least and where you least expect it, there will be happiness waiting for you.

But always remember to be aware of all the details that allow you to retain happiness at his side as much as you can, if you ever lose happiness, hurry to start immediately a recovery plan of happiness, not wasting energy lamenting or complaining about the loss suffered, positively channeled that energy to seek happiness again and this time, make sure it is forever.

"The secret of happiness is not always doing what you want, but always want what you do". Leo Nikolayevich Tolstoy, Russian writer. Thanks to the literary movement of realism is considered one of the most important writers of world literature.

Ninth day: Hope brings prosperity

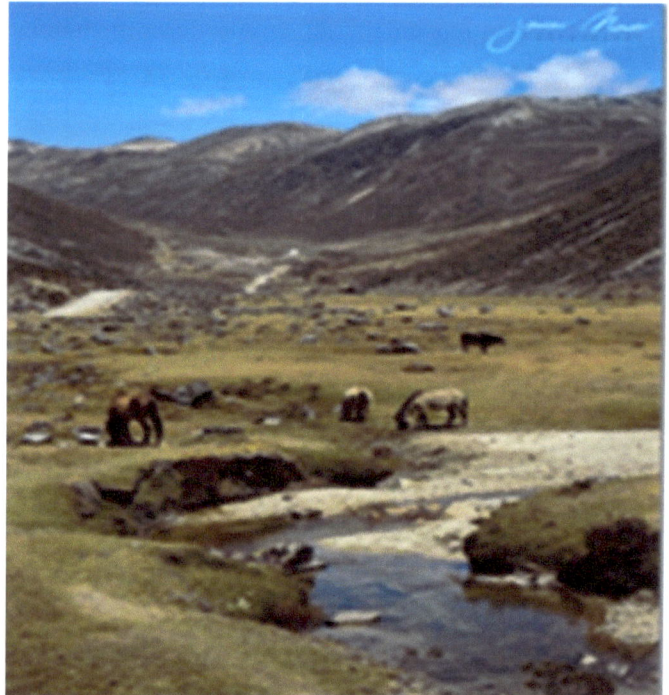

Sharing The Park; Merida, Venezuela.

As a rainbow brightening the day after the storm hope so, after stirring always calm returns, perspective and hope for a better life, full of happiness and lasting harmony.

Once past the bad time which has been submitted, try to immediately attracts with you prosperity, clinging to hope like a frightened child to her mother clings, but you should know that prosperity is manifested in many ways and not necessarily refers to the increase in economic capital which almost always associate.

Hope allows you to focus on the blessings that you receive and that soon thanks to his conviction those blessings fall from heaven for you, will be bigger and more followed.

To notice them should thank the Universe immediately by each of the blessings received and prepared with proper behavior and humble attitude to receive more and better blessings, until you can live with yours in abundance and satisfaction; physical, spiritual and financial.

It is true that perhaps at some point in their life, by a twist of fate, you will lose everything: family, work, money, property, health, spiritual and emotional tranquility, but the last thing we should not lose under any circumstances is Hope and if this happens, you must urgently return to try to keep in mind the hope in her life, because she and only she will, the impulse that moves everything necessary to bring prosperity again, is similar to that you launch a fact a pool and not know how to swim, sinks to bottom out, and then you just need to be encouraged to go back up and that will be his only salvation, so just acts: Hope

"The hope is to be able to see the light despite all the darkness" Desmond Mpilo Tutu. Pacifist South African. He earned his Nobel peace work, Unesco and International Awards Catalonia.

Tenth day: Understanding the Faith.

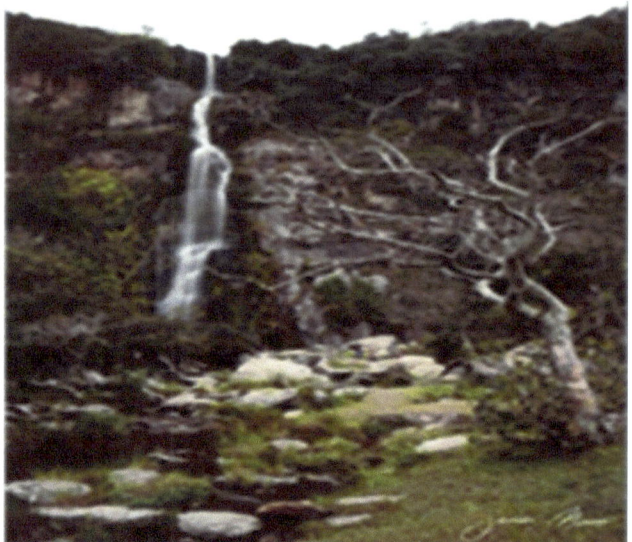

Giving life, Waterfall Wine; Lara, Venezuela.

You should be aware at all times that if you ask for something, anything; so it seems impossible to reach, but asks with absolute faith, must prepare to receive it, because with complete security will manifest in the way that most benefits you and yours, but not necessarily in the way that you want.

When you understand that it must act with faith in something or something, observed as advances with safe passage and confidently towards what you want, every step forward will be firmer than before, with more strength, safety and wisdom to achieve progress constantly without any fear, when you feel uncertainty in some stretches of the road, quieted the thoughts and soon feel that return to the road more firmly, because their faith is the supreme power that accompanies it and if we ever hoards going to leave .

An old and popular saying goes "Faith moves mountains," was drawn from the biblical quotation from Matthew 17:20 that says, "Jesus said, I assure you that if you have faith so be it small as a mustard seed, you can tell a mountain Move from here to there and be moved. For those of you with faith nothing it will be impossible "; and it is not literally a say; is certainly, with authentic faith, you will be able to move any obstacle the size of a mountain, and make something good happen or something bad will not happen. With true faith and complete conviction, everything you ask will move you, even if the load is bigger and heavier than a mountain.

"Faith covers the invisible, knows the limitations of the senses; also transcends the limits of human reason, the processes of nature, the specific terms of the experience." St. Bernard of Clairvaux. religious holy French.

Eleventh day: Pray for others.

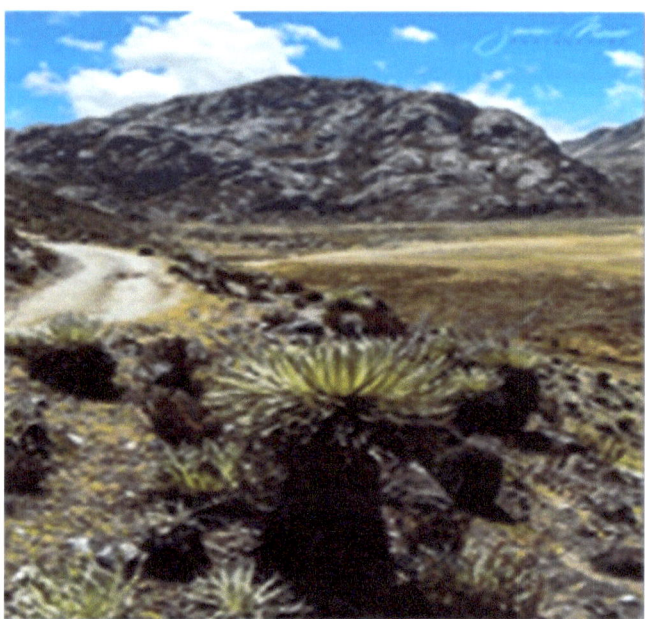

The dome; Merida, Venezuela.

When you pray to the Upper Force in which he believes, whatever; with all his being but with humility and sincerity, feels a liberating energy flows through your body and your mind, whether you do it because it has been planned as a daily ritual or because as many of us do, we pray when we are in times of difficulties, but the truth is that the simple act of faith, used to ward off any fears and see more clearly the problems and concerns that you face in life and so that they can be faced in the best way possible.

When you pray for others, and share their faith and their spiritual energies, says the supreme power and channel energies that perhaps one in his concern cannot channel for good.

Pray for others, it is an act that guarantees reward since sometime also many others pray for you and that will make a collective force capable of transforming, with faith and hope, their world, the world of their own, the world of others and the world of all, to the relief of the needs and abundant obtaining benefit and collective prosperity.

Praying for others, it's just the beginning of a collective indestructible chain Fe, strong and unbreakable chain of personal protection and not the will never break any evil force and providing prosperity, blessings and health for you, so will for others, which inevitably improve the world in which we live.

"Prayer is the Babbling who believes. The war cry of the believer who struggle and the requiem of the dying saint who sleeps in the arms of the Lord. It is the air we breathe is the secret key, is the breath, the strength and the privilege of every human being". Charles Haddon Spurgeon. British Baptist Minister. Who evangelize more than 10 million people is known worldwide as the Prince of Preachers.

Twelfth day: Service to others.

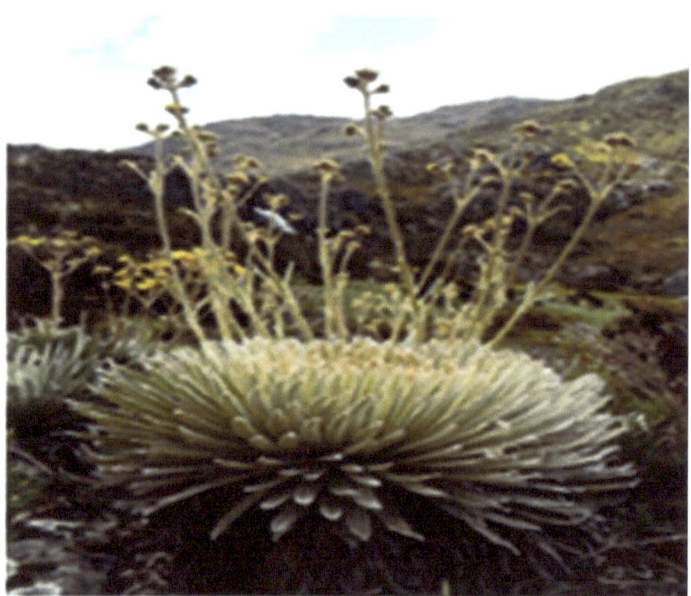

Frailejón; Mérida, Venezuela.

If you dedicate your life to serving others, be assured that you will be blessed forever and many will rate their dedication and hard work, but especially if it does so without expecting anything in return, you cannot avoid receiving divine reward.

All mankind significantly appreciate who serves and serves for good without expecting anything in return, but a Superior Force will be the most valued and rewarded their selfless efforts.

At no time you should worry because someone thought a fool by the fact serve that is in need of help, because for him that really matters, never go for a fool, now that his actions show mercy, selflessness and understanding for others.

No need to form a great foundation to help or devote full time to charity abandoning their responsibilities, a simple daily gesture of help, however simple it may be, is like the passing of a comet on a dark night, a simple smile to someone this in sorrow that person can trigger a series of feelings that can ease the pain and improve your day.

"Help the child who needs you, that child will partner with your child. It helps old and young will help when you are. Service to others is a secure happiness as enjoying the nature and care for to come. It gives without measure and give you beyond measure." Facundo Cabral (Rodolfo Enrique Cabral), Singer-Songwriter, Argentine composer, social critic.

Thirteenth day: Letting go of something better will come.

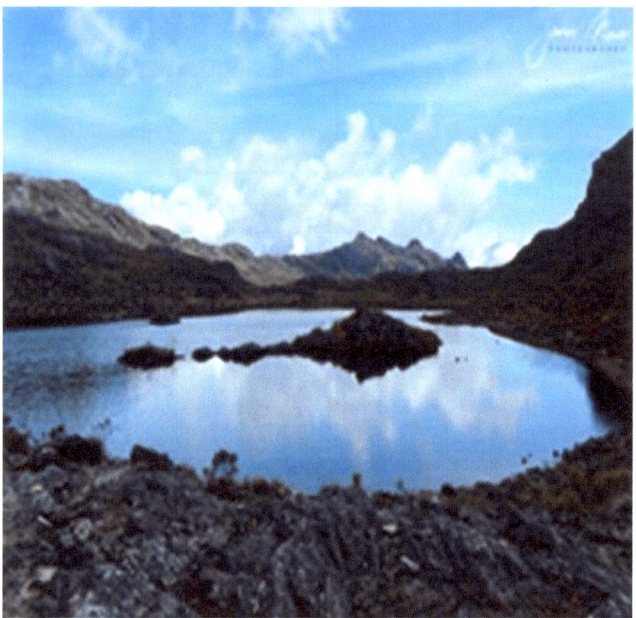

Islet of Santo Cristo; Merida, Venezuela.

When confronted with a situation in which you have to decide to let go of the comfortable or acquaintance, leaving your comfort zone, it's natural to feel a great fear of what comes from the fact of being an unknown situation, a situation similar to living a paratrooper before making his first leap, is paralyzed for a few moments, you are not sure what to do, even thought in those moments of doubt backtrack; but we say with certainty that final step with faith; With great faith, trusting that the upper force immediately replace that fear with excitement to fully enjoy the new experience that has just started.

Let go and trust fully in that Superior Force in which you believe; whatever way you perceive it, it allows you to avoid worrying about an uncertain and unexpected result and instead will be sure that everything will be better than you have expected.

Remember to fully trust, better and more exciting soon come to life and will surely be the best that can happen.

But if by letting go, come back to you someday, just it was always yours and will now be a better and more rewarding experience than most never lose. But it becomes; and we affirm it, something will come better because you're ready for bigger and better blessings every day.

"You can be happy if you are willing to let go of your past and get rid of the obstacles to fly". Chris Prentiss. Writer. American. Founder of training centers for rehabilitation of people with addictions.

Fourteenth day: The flow of life.

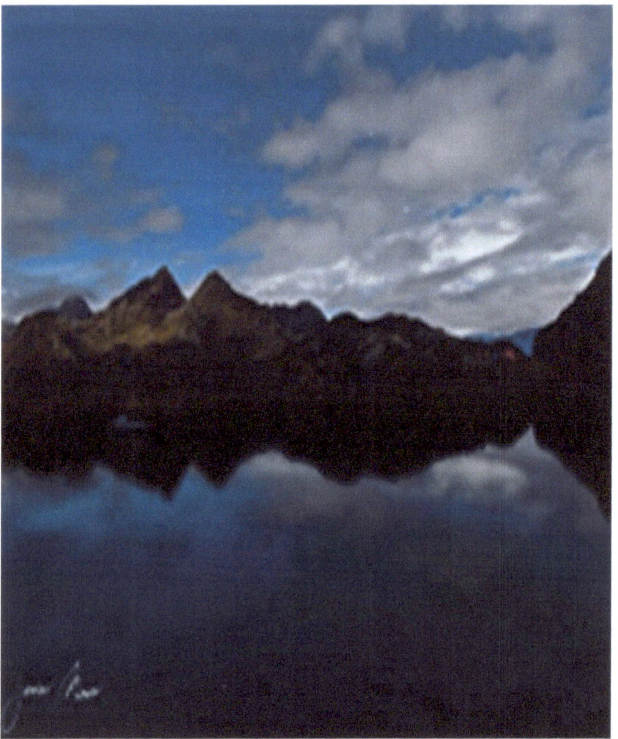

Lake Indigo night; Merida, Venezuela.

And is convinced that the body and mind are pure energy that is not destroyed but instead always remains with us in constant flux and transformation, regardless of appearances or external constraints, all things work together for the welfare if positively channels energy, for it must express positive thoughts, concrete and correct actions to achieve make your life in this world full of blessings trip.

Observe at all times special attention to your body and mind because of them energy flows constantly, observe carefully the signals it sends you so that the energy flow positively as he who lights a campfire and achieved in a short time high flare and strong, so you must act.

The great mathematician and Greek astronomer Erastóteles to determine the dimensions of planet Earth drawing on the implementation of a trigonometric method defined by himself and the inclusion of the terms of latitude and longitude, concluded among other things; that there was but a single system; The universe, everything else was sub-systems that made this unique system called Universe and therefore you are also part of a sub-system of the universe, by definition part of the universe and as such should be allowed to flow his life harmoniously within the greater universe, providing with correct actions and decisions their bit for the Universe to walk in peace and harmony while his life is in constant progress and harmony.

"How you can own water really? Always flowing in the flow, it is never the same, which trace the flow of life. Because life is a constant flow." James Joyce (James Augustine Aloysius Joyce). Irish writer, a prominent representative of the current literary vanguard.

Fifteenth day: Healing energy.

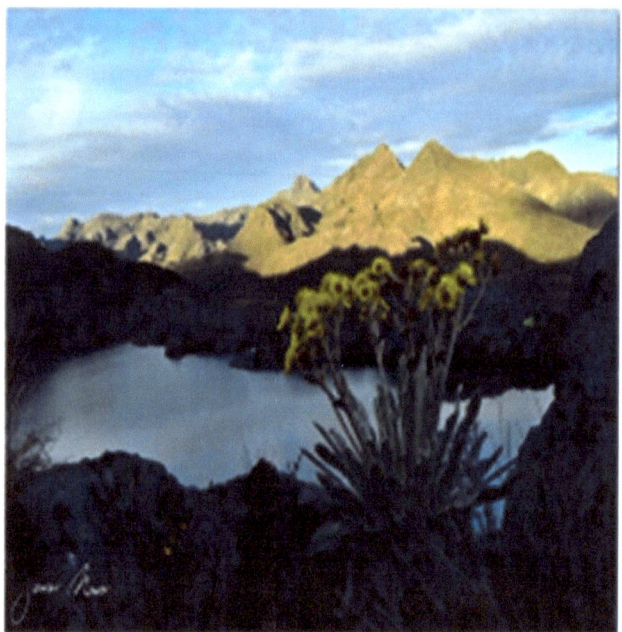

Lake Indigo; Mérida, Venezuela.

we are convinced that we are energy and we are both part of a superior force, also known by the law of conservation of energy, that it cannot be destroyed, it can only be changed from one form to another; is that all energy can be transformed, use this proven principle of physics to improve, treat yourself peace; concentrate and meditate, enjoy moments of serenity to restore and repair your mind and spirit, it is also scientifically proven that absolutely all the cells that make up each organs that make up our body has the ability to regenerate, is called cell regeneration process that simply changing eating habits and the way of seeing life get perfect health.

Remember control breathing as a vital tool to properly oxygenate all organs, breathe slowly and deeply, inhale and exhale watching with full awareness as each breath air filled the total capacity of the lungs while each exhalation contemplated as expels his body all disease and negative thinking, drink plenty of water at least four liters per day so you detoxify your body while the cells meet in better shape cell exchange necessary for the proper functioning of the body and mind, keep in mind that staying hydrated prevents heart attacks, improves digestion, reduces the risk of colon, bladder or breast cancer and keeps the skin healthy and young.

Exercise your body constantly with a lot of discipline, walk at least three times a week, for not less than one hour with this simple routine you activate your circulatory system, remember to always walk at the same speed to avoid injury while does not alter your heart rate, note that walks you do for work issues are not the same healthy effects on you, because your body is predisposed at that time it is a job, a responsibility to fulfill and no so an activity of recreation and enjoyment.

When you walk close to nature admire the beauty around him, thanks to the Universe because there is this wonderful creation, leave that moment all the worries away from you, put your mind blank and just admire even the smallest of details, so you can constantly flowing healing energy that revitalizes and restores.

The healing energy is within ourselves, ready always receive positive instructions from us to re-patterning, such as computer software, contact her through her thoughts and emotions, which should always be optimistic, to achieve and strengthen your immune system and thus prevent any disease.

Keep in mind; like any computer software, healing energy is also exposed to the attack of the "computer virus", which in this case is nothing more than the constant bombardment that you are subjected daily by the average of alarmist, media, multinational companies pharmaceutical, which for profit deify the disease and medication, and the envious neighbor who tells you that illness, misfortune and problems are present at all times. How we not are going to be prone to illness? When all we hear, talk and think it is related to diseases.

Fortunately; there is a healing energy, present in our DNA waiting for quantum instructions, willing to communicate with our cellular structure so we can shield our immune systems shooing all kinds of disease.

"In every culture and in every medical tradition before ours, healing was accomplished by moving energy." Albert Szent-Gyorgyl. Hungarian physician, Nobel Prize in Medicine.

Sixteen day: Healing presence.

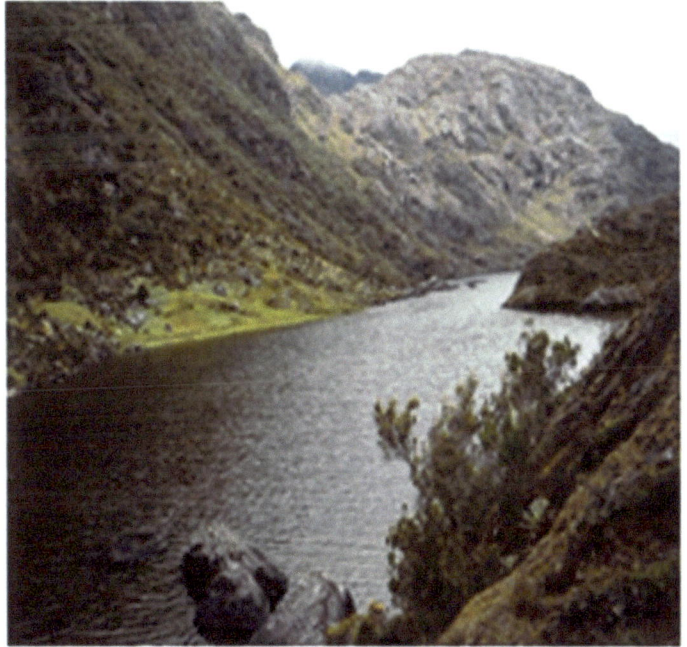

Laguna El Hoyo; Mérida, Venezuela.

The healing presence is manifested in many ways and does not have a certain time, healing usually the most difficult, is not a physical illness but of a wounded heart, but should know; Faith that leads you to a healing presence to come to you and heal all their wounds, because the most enduring and vital health is the soul.

A healthy soul, does not accept the presence of fear, anxiety or worry, when you let yourself take by such disturbances body reflects and manifests immediately appear diseases "itis": gastritis, rhinitis, tonsillitis, arthritis, etc., which damage the body and life.

To live to the fullest every day.

Keep healthy your soul, feel the healing presence and progressively disappear any disease or ailment. Remember the words of the Greek sage Socrates: "the joy of the soul, forms the beautiful days of life" and this cannot doubt because he said nothing more than one of the world's great philosophers of all time.

"There is no medicine to cure what no cure happiness", Gabriel García Márquez, Colombian writer, Nobel Literature Premium.

Tenth seventh day: The best of you.

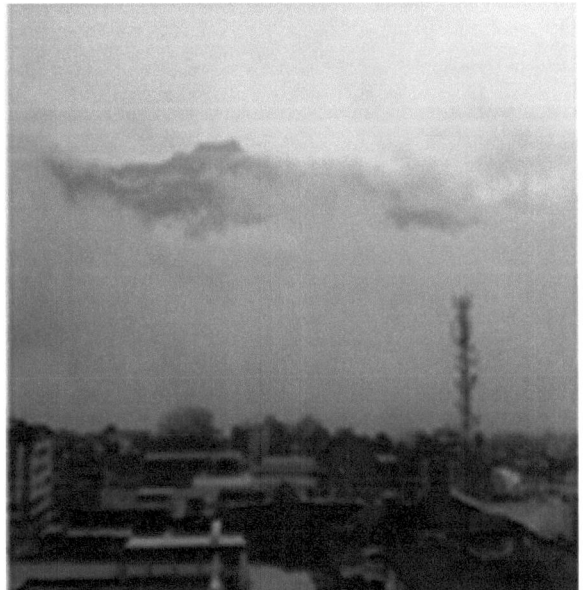

Mist; Mérida, Venezuela.

Never compare yourself with others for more admiration you have them, just take the references that are important and that will serve as a guide to improve your life, progress every day, remember that your achievements and victories are scored on the giant chessboard of the universe, appreciate their efforts and talents that comments from people who judge without reason, because very possibly because they deem to be convinced that they have the ability to be what you are or have achieved in life.

Convince yourself that if you pay more attention to the up building things he has done and to be done, strives to reinforce their strengths and abilities, your life will be easier and more enjoyable.

To live to the fullest every day.

Make the most of all their strengths and skills to advance and prosper in your life, remember an old popular saying that goes: "If the sky will fall lemons make lemonade," Be strong and do not place more excuses between success and you once you start executing all its actions with sincere faith, will see how everything flows to achieve the goals it has set, follow undismayed by this path and see them as opportunities to grow all the obstacles that are presented on the road, but yes; You must be willing to do their best and maximum effort every day to achieve

"If you have a positive attitude and constantly struggles to give your best effort, eventually going to overcome your immediate problems and find you're ready for bigger challenges." Pat Riley (Patrick Riley) Basketball coach six times NBA champion maximum professional basketball tournament in the world.

Eighteen day: Turn on your light.

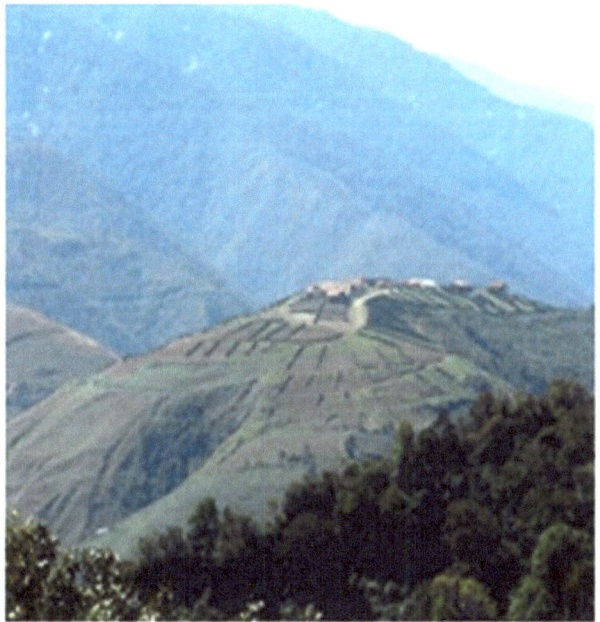

Plateaus in Tabay; Mérida, Venezuela.

If our whole body is full of energy and that energy can be converted into light, you should know that our whole body is full of light, therefore no room for gloom and darkness, will emanate in all light moment that illuminates everything around you, you must learn to project it as a lamp that illuminates the night with her light, trust that inner light that comes from your spirit to show the right way to go.

When you feel that life becomes complicated, then on with greater intensity the inner light that with its moral and ethical actions, go around the track guiding the family and younger with the assurance that they will in right direction the happiness.

To live to the fullest every day.

It should be clear that your right action, achieve spiritual and personal growth, which will make your inner light shine more brightly and maybe some people around you feel uncomfortable by that fact, but always acts with love, showing kindness and understanding, surely will correct any problems and allow you to continue your way in peace.

The light emanating enlighten yours way, the family and the youngest, but be careful that the light emitted from your being not dazzles others fills the heart with compassion and humility than ever that light stop light your mind and your life.

"In you the world light is the only light. If you are unable to see it in yourself, it is useless to look elsewhere." Mabel Collins. English novelist, prominent Theosophical.

Ninetieth day: Walk with your family.

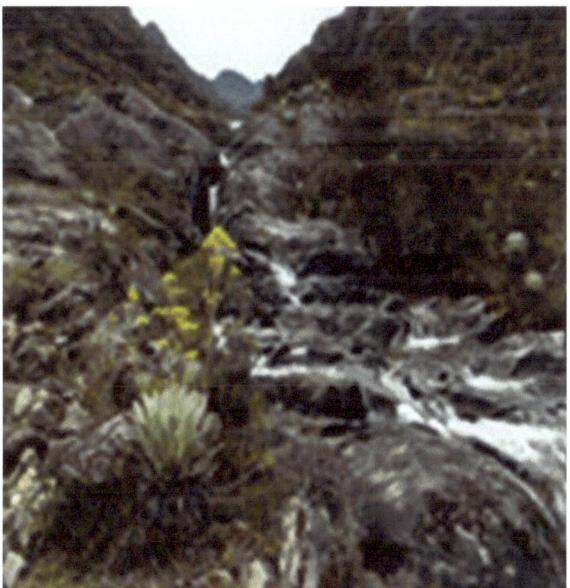

Rising lagoon El Hoyo, Mérida- Venezuela.

Treasure every moment to share with his family, true friends and childhood friends; fully enjoy them, place them above anything else, deliver all the time they deserve; do not be stingy, because those are the moments of genuine happiness, take advantage to remove accumulated daily stress, worry and anxiety that may cause the problems faced in their daily activities.

Take advantage of those moments for family members especially children be approached and convert those moments reflective, flexible and responsive periods, always greet your loved ones with love, whatever the circumstances by which you or they are going.

To live to the fullest every day.

For family and yours, always has to be prepared in the best way possible, offer your help, your support, your solidarity, because the family is always family, in all circumstances to live, even if they at some point give back, his family will remain forever and it is your responsibility continue to support them.

Try to start a project of any kind with yours, incorporate them into the formulation of ideas, by posing their own or give life to their ideas, guide them, support and is its leader as the great father, guide projects to fruition, remember that companies family are one of the most important in the world of global business options, while on an adventure of entrepreneurship beside his draw in your mind forever a beautiful memory.

"Do not walk ahead of me, I may not follow you. Do not walk behind me, you cannot guide you. Walk beside me and be my friend. " Albert Camus. Novelist and playwright French that reflected the philosophy of the absurd.

Twentieth day: Enjoy your freedom responsibly.

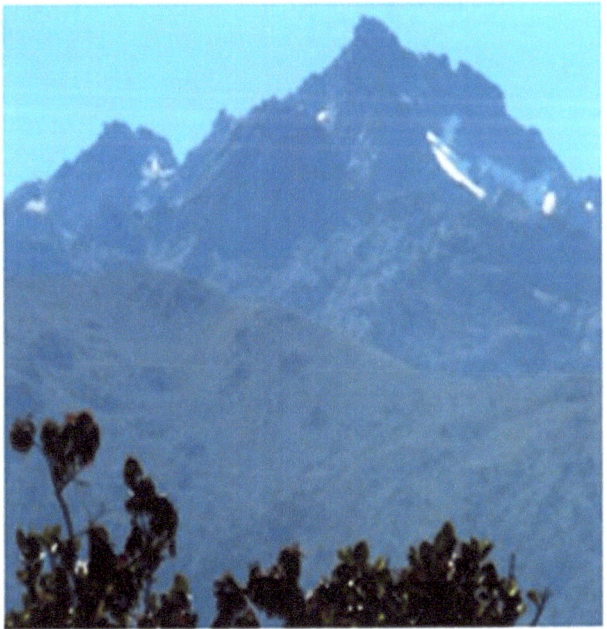

Pico Bolívar; Mérida, Venezuela.

Freedom is the essence of being, you are free to do whatever you want; even should all do what we want before depart this level, but know you; that freedom has a limit, which is respect for others and the obligation not affect either the nature or others in transit through your constant pursuit of freedom for your mind, spirit and body.

You are free to change, free to grow and try to do their duty day. Grow day by day should be your motto of life; grow spiritually and intellectually without realizing you will be free in spirit. At all times of your life should be fully aware of this undeniable truth.

To live to the fullest every day.

Remember that anyone or anything, under any circumstances, may put strings to a free spirit.

Use your freedom to do well at all times and to meet all your aims, make an inventory of the plans at any time of his life proposed, no matter what time you have to have raised it, nor unusual they may seem, separate the aims that could not meet and make a list; order him according to their current priorities and start from now to develop a plan to achieve them one after another is steady and not lose heart.

"Freedom, Sancho, is one of the most precious gifts that the men gave the heavens; with it not can compare treasures that enclose the land and sea; for freedom and for honor, one can and should risk one's life." Miguel de Cervantes Saavedra. Spanish writer, extract its world famous work Don Quixote.

Twenty-first day: You will always be protected.

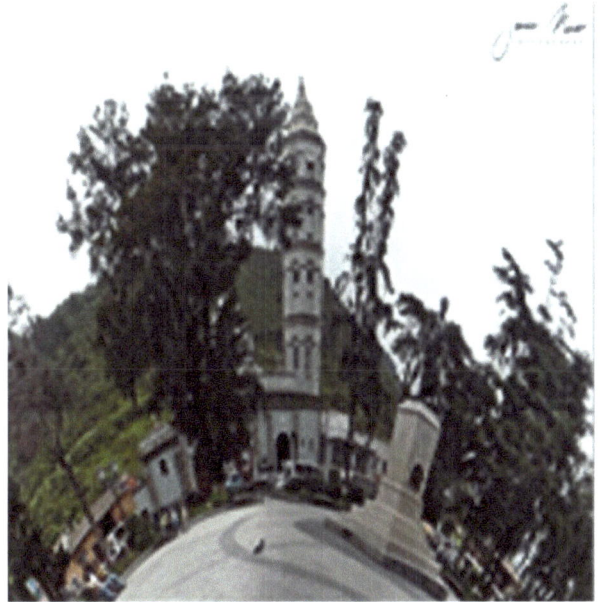

Square Bolívar; Timotes, Venezuela.

The entire universe is constantly protecting you and your loved ones, must bear this in mind and should always trust that it is, when you are worried for any reason or in an unexpected situation that generates anxiety, recognize the presence of light and love the Upper Force which manifests itself in the vastness of the universe, whatever the way in which you perceive immediately will calm your mind, trust fully and feel safe, secure and protected in any negative situation you experience.

Stay tuned for warning signs that manifest themselves in an unexpected situation, you may be in a dream, in a "hunch" in an inner voice that speaks to him, even in mild illness such as a fever, because that fever you He considers it a disease, is nothing more than a defense mechanism which appeals body, face a greater threat and likewise are the warning signs that always protect against any threat.

To live to the fullest every day.

Nevertheless; if you do not pay attention to these warning signals or not able to decipher, yet generous universe around him tend a fence to protect you, your family and your belongings, because he trusted and did so with faith.

"When the deepest anguish emerges the faint but firm certainty that everything that happens is not so real, that beyond fear there is a protection there somewhere unknown protects us." Pierre Lemaitre, French writer winner, excerpt from his work Goncourt Prize: Wedding Dress.

Twenty second day: The consolation will be present.

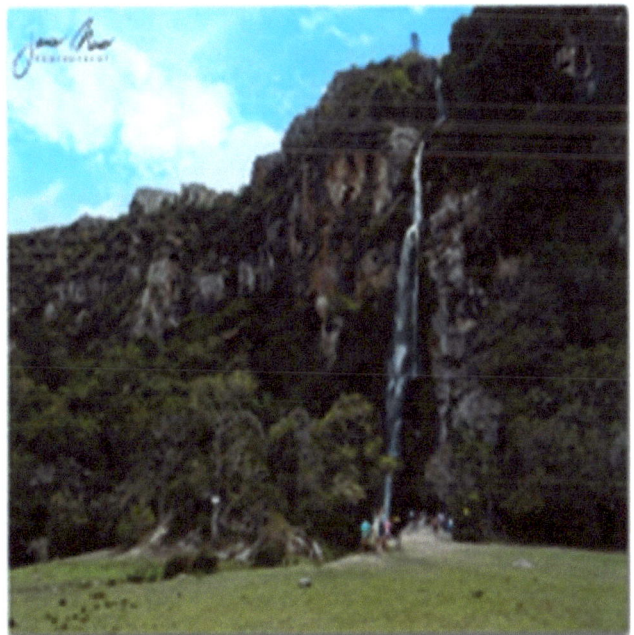

Waterfall Wine; Lara, Venezuela.

In life going through difficult times is inevitable, perhaps the permanent loss of a loved one is for most of us the most devastating moment of life, in situations like these, receives compression generous comfort that certainly will come from the hand of a loved one, a complete stranger or even be surprised perhaps his worst enemy.

Nevertheless; You must know something, that there is a Higher Force which we have discussed before, which is always ready to comfort and protect at any time of distress or sadness. Understand that you certainly will not find a better comfort for their afflictions if your life governs absolute faith.

To live to the fullest every day.

The Upper Force, will act as did his mother when he was a child, desperately running with you when most needed, fully open inside to receive it, immerse yourself in total silence and see how soon feel the love and protection of that Upper strength.

Once fully revive coincide in stating that the Upper Force is always ready to come to your aid when you need it and never hesitate to attend always that presents an unexpected situation.

"In the multitude of my thoughts within me. Your consolations rejoice my soul. " King David. Salm 94; the holy Bible.

Twenty-third day: Tranquility, you most precious treasure.

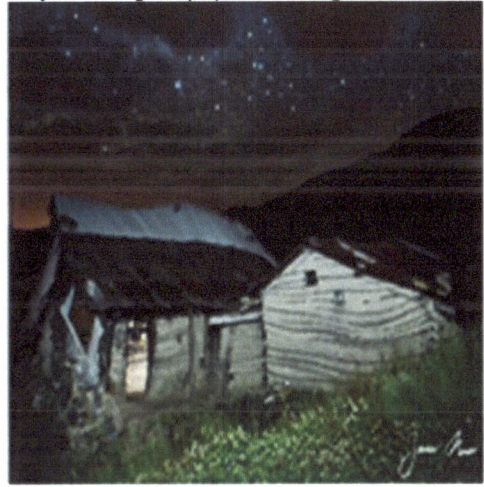

Rancho under the moon, Loma Verde; Táchira, Venezuela.

Always try to act correctly, without harming others and most importantly without harming you, do not alter the course of things using for this lies, cheating and deception, remember that the best will always come, so do not despair or lose faith, not violate their moral principles, divine or legal norms. Well, if violent the normal course of life with deceptions, you will have peace of mind or body, or the soul; remember to always get up fresh and rejuvenated after sleeping peacefully, to enjoy the reflection in a serene place surrounded by the most beautiful nature, share with your loved ones a pleasant evening enjoying an appetizing menu, see in their children that look of joy and pride to be with you, only achieved and enjoyed if his body and soul are fully in state of tranquility and that is only possible through proper actions for life.

"It's not wealth nor splendor, but tranquility and occupation which give you happiness." Thomas Jefferson, politician, lawyer, third President of the United States of America.

Twenty-fourth day: Guide your way.

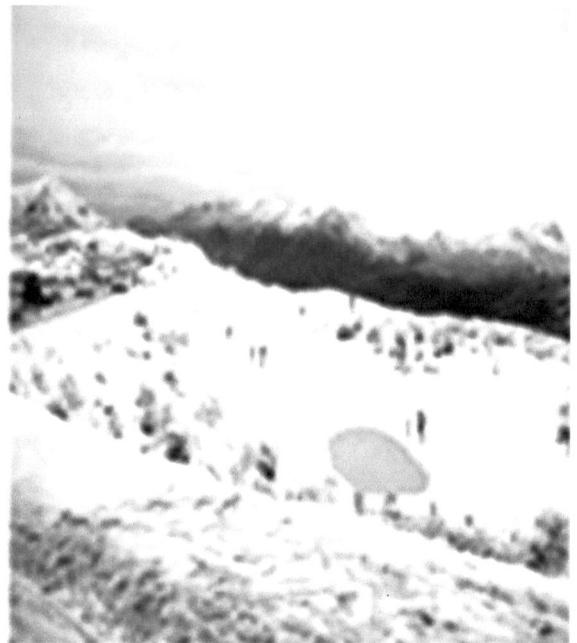

Pico El Águila; Mérida, Venezuela.

As the Magi followed the star of Bethlehem, trusting no doubt whatsoever that would lead them to their destination, so you must follow the path to your objectives, guided by the light that illuminates life, stay attentive to warning signs they manifest in your way, always remember that each new challenge to undertake, there are countless opportunities, although not the wait and every difficulty that confronts it keeps a nice reward.

Write in mind and on paper their life plan to follow, divide it into three parts: the first short-term objectives you want to achieve in the next 90 days, then scores the objectives and targets in the medium term place them between 90 days and one year and finally record the long term; those who take to get over a year.

Ensure that the vast majority of the objectives are interrelated, reaching a objectives short ground you term basis to achieve the target over the medium term and then long-term, do not forget to constantly assess progress, obstacles and delays that occur in each period, write without leaving aside any details all evolution of their life plan and firm objectivity consider new possibilities arising achievements; I tested the tools available and that besides the support they get from others to achieve each goal requires finally; be very sincere in detail the risks that you must address, type an alternate plan for each situation that expresses fully rely on their abilities and not faint to successfully reach the final objectives set.

Step by Step; without forcing the course of events but also without neglecting at any time comply with the layout in your life plan, periodically review what has been done, analyzing how to improve and solve problems as they arise, in this way; the way of your life plan will lead exactly to achieve all your objectives.

But it should be aware that you have to use correctly above all, the five key elements that guarantee the successful development of any project and of course in a life plan.

Organization: You must start developing a methodology to be followed strictly by you and your team in case of need to contemplate, it will do, how, when, with what resources, with whom and for what it will do. And I develop for each objective as it arises.

Discipline: Perform step by step all activities pose to achieve the objectives set in their life plan, as I put it and respecting the exact times that you assigned to each task.

Cleaning: Cleaning not only refers to neatness in each of the elements involved in their life plan, or cleaning should seek at all times in infrastructure, furniture and neatness of his presence, but more importantly ; remove all the old, what trouble, what nonfunctional, including first; your old negative beliefs. To start from scratch, without any defect or wrong experience.

Punctuality: Begin, develop and conclude all deadlines in the desired time, for that you must consider the importance of the organization again, because the methodology you are going to implement, should analyze the execution times of activities that take you to the goals set.

Commitment: You and all your team must be ready at all times to make the issues raised with faith and perseverance undismayed at any time once they begin.

"It is bold and astute in your plans, firm, steady, persevering in the implementation and decided to find a glorious end." Major General Carl Philipp Gottlieb von Clausewitz, one of the most influential historians and theorists of modern military science. Extract of his work: Beginning of the war.

Twenty fifth day: Willing to everything.

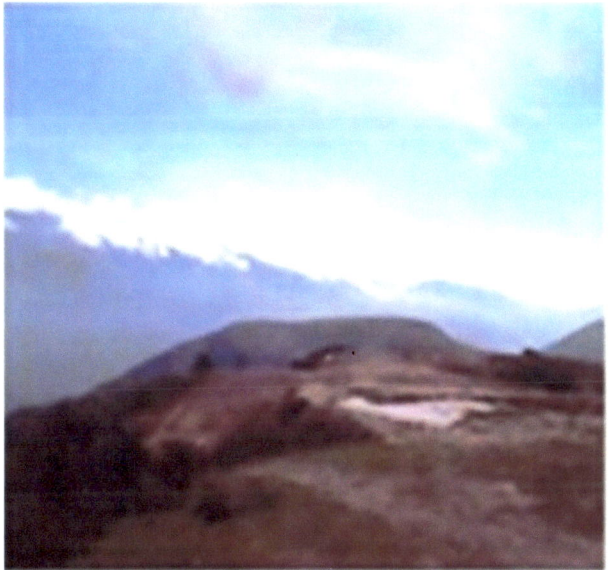

From Southern village; Mérida, Venezuela.

Must be willing to everything always and everywhere, yes willing to consider and make everything legal, permissive and morally right, according to their beliefs and what dictates your common sense, you should know that any change in his life for the least it is, begins with the willingness and determination you have to do it.

The arrangement with discipline define the ability to make changes or corrections, if you expect something different in life, you must be willing to work in what has never worked, forgive what has not forgiven, allow what is not allowed, share what has not shared act as he never acted, though: whenever legal, permissive and morally correct.

To live to the fullest every day.

Whether to change your lifestyle, to improve or to continue living life as he is living, must always be ready for anything, to make every day the best of their ability, as in a soccer game, fight to the last minute, for perhaps 90 minutes more additional minutes added by the referee, you get the victory. So mysterious, fascinating and splendid is the wonderful game, in which he had to be the main star: **YOUR LIFE.**

"Do not be afraid to give up the good to go so great," John Davison Rockefeller. Entrepreneur, investor, founder of Standard Oil, the oil company that controlled 90% of US oil.

Twenty-sixth day: Arm yourself with courage

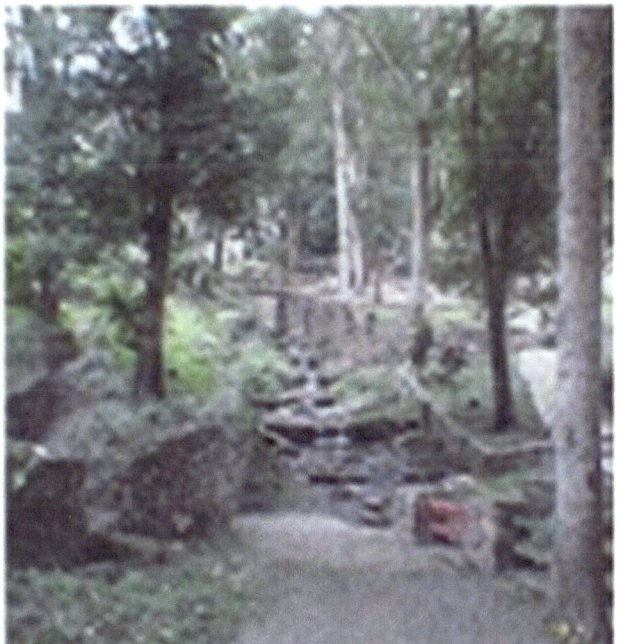

Park The Illustrious; Trujillo, Venezuela.

From now on; arm yourself with courage, because if you cannot control your taste each of the circumstances that are presented in life, what is certain is that it must have the courage to choose how to perceive, act and respond to those circumstances.

If a negative moment occurs, you must have the courage to face it with confidence, attitude and positive thinking, confident that with discipline, order and planning properly will overcome this difficulty.

You have to be encouraged, and strive fearlessly express value to the events of life by more negative than these are, trying to take advantage and benefit at all times.

To live to the fullest every day.

Remember that you have the blessing of being able to decide in any situation of life, for this you have two alternatives, taking it as a positive learning experience or a negative that is sure going to sink more. But only you decide and you alone are responsible for the decision taken.

Is in you, it depends exclusively: **Arm yourself with courage.**

"The real value is to advance all the dangers and despise when they get to be inevitable," Francois Fenelon, French theologian writer and author of the famous adventures of Telemachus.

Twenty seventh day: Ready for action.

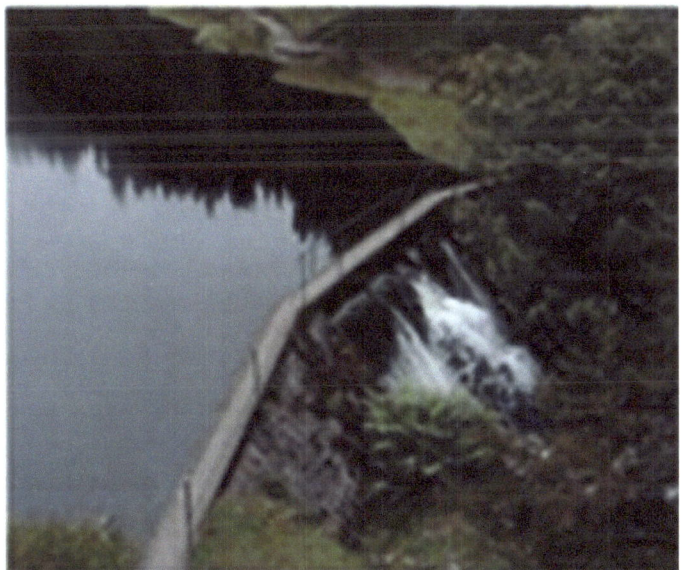

Lagoon Victoria; Mérida, Venezuela.

Look very well in the image that identifies this day, as stated in the footnote of it, corresponds to the Lagoon Victoria, beautiful natural scenery located in the wastelands of Los Andes in Venezuela, specifically in Merida state.

However; imagine for a moment that is fleeing an armed murderer because of bad circumstances, will run across the bridge to all that their physical capabilities allow, just when you think you will achieve reach the other end of the bridge, at the end of it it is another murderer waiting and holding a gun, his reaction is to stop immediately, we assure you that the only thing that will scared is to look to the waterfall and a second later launched without thinking about much else and without considering the consequences that this act will it can generate.

It is regrettable that so surely you act at all times in his life; waiting for an external stimulus of course, not as alarming as this you just tell; but if waiting for something to happen to act foreign to you, it rains heavily to run like a sprinter athlete who will shout to power your body, which abruptly wake up so early morning is.

We will never allow more. Always be ready at all times for action, because life is an adventure, which should and is obliged to live each day to the fullest; it is also the best adventures or probably the only adventure possible.

"The maximum sample of what a human being is not how you react in moments of comfort and convenience, but how it behaves in times of challenge and controversy" Dr. Martin Luther King Jr. Civil Rights Activist, Nobel Prize Peace.

Twenty-eighth day: Respect the Divine Order.

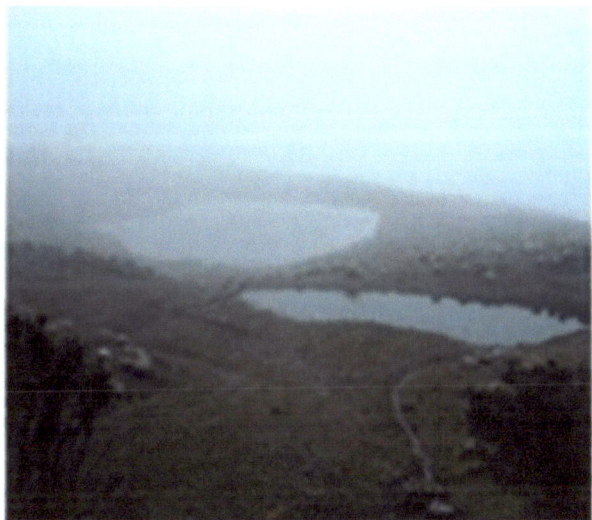

Lagunas del Páramo; Mérida, Venezuela.

Believe it or not, everything works because there is a divine order, are millions of years to reach this point and have the privilege of being summoned for this adventure called life, which took so long to organize.

Now you have the privilege, the greatest honor of all; live and enjoy life, either as live or how you live, but it is for a short time and do not even have information on the exact moment we just life.

So only respects the divine order, knowing that everything has its cause and effect, be aware that this cause has a flow that should not be placed resistance, enjoying peace, balance the body and spirit, seeks daily gain wisdom, exercise both body and mind, eat healthy, work, rest, sleep well, share with your family and above all always remember that you are an important part of the divine order of life.

Divine order is present in every moment of our lives, whether that things are calm or agitated, even in those moments when things are incomprehensible, it should be clear that everything works for a reason that has to do with reality that next to every human life or not, it is expressed and is simply divine order.

The fact accept unequivocally leads us to walk the path of peace and harmony.

"Faith: The certainty of knowing that everything is in Divine Order and trust." Alice Ramos. Sociologist.

Twenty ninth day: Discipline guarantees success.

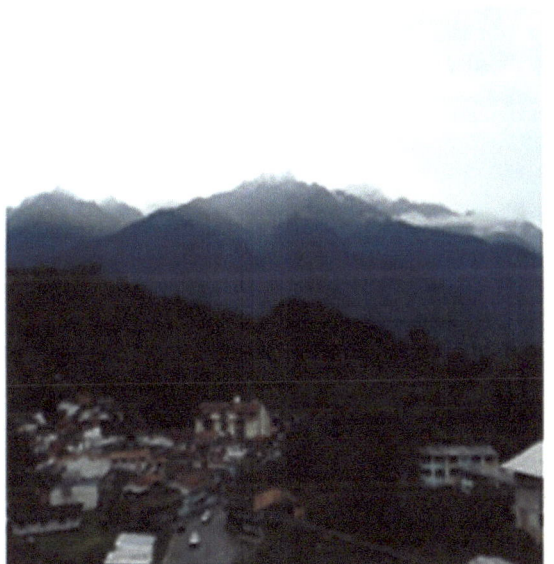

View from work; Mérida, Venezuela.

If you have come this far reading, following the instructions that are embodied at the beginning of this writing, firmly believes that it has exponentially improved their life, not because reading what we express you enjoyed much or because he thought the worst thing that has I read in your life, either because they believe it or not read; it is only your decision, simply because of something much more important than all this is that you my dear friend had: **Discipline.**

Discipline allowed us to achieve all the objectives that we draw to us in life. All you've proposed whatever the term was drawn and whatever the difficulties encountered along the way to reach them.

Discipline has shown to reach the objectives of reading this book, is the same to be followed in every action you take in your life from now on.

With **discipline** safely supplanting any weakness or lack possessing to achieve an objectives and eventually you will realize how insignificant it was that lack.

With **Discipline**, achieved everything that is proposed in this life and can firmly tell everyone that came into this world: **to live to the fullest every day.**

Remember that discipline is the ability to act orderly and perseveringly for an achievement, keep discipline in your life, at work and note that progressed rapidly and continuously.

"Discipline strengthens the mind to be impervious to the corrosive influence fear." Bernard Law Montgomery. US Marshal Field in World War II.

Thirtieth day: Search and find.

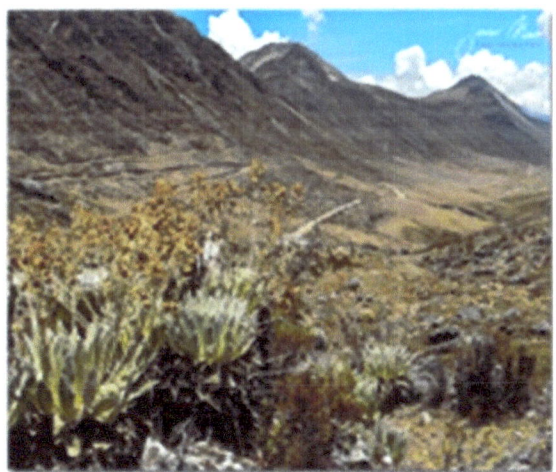

Valley Mifafi, Mérida- Venezuela.

On this day we assure you that this questioning many things, perhaps meditating or perhaps rectify demanding, but he knows he wants and needs change some aspect in your life no matter how small. Be aware that you need to look for something else to achieve its full realization. Not care what urges seek: peace, strength, new life, new challenges, no matter what the reason, but already you convinced that you have thousands of blessings, which emanates from you a powerful positive energy and is on the way right to achieve happiness, which from now an obstacle that this is not an impediment but a message to correct, because what look you find.

"Do not let anyone tell you that you are unable to do something. If you have a dream you should keep it. If you want something go get it. People who cannot get their dreams often tell others that neither meets theirs". Will Smith, actor, acting like millionaire Chis Gardner, enterprising American speaker. In the film "Pursuit of happiness".

Thirty-first day: one with God.

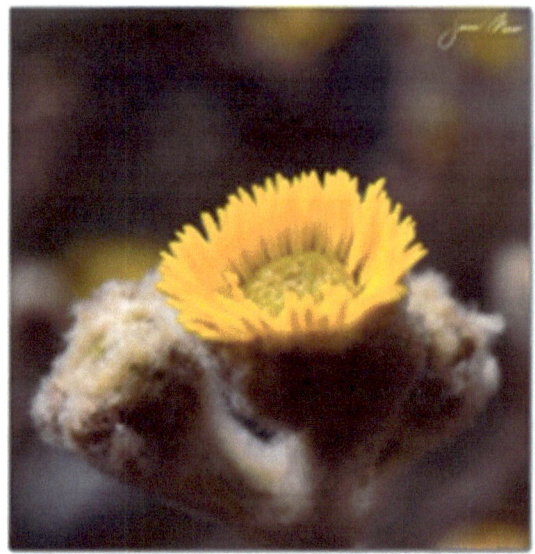

Rebirth

We have made this point so that you read the last day of each month, whether the month ending in 28, 29, 30 or 31, because you should know to be one with **God**, it is a feeling, is everything and the only thing reassures your soul, one with **God**, it's your soul itself, it is life itself. Being one with **God**, in whatever form they know it, recognize it and accept it, it is the full knowledge of your inner being.

Acknowledge your oneness with **God** and you will be convinced that you will never be alone and instead have with you at all times the best companies, the best partner and most faithful friend, you will always protect the one you nurses, providing you security, love and peace in all situations of your life.

"Because you are one with God, you are part of it and be aware of that reality, that is the key to live to the fullest every day." Daniel Gomez. The Author.